TENOR SAX

101 DISNEY SONGS

Note: The keys in this book do not match the other wind instruments.

Available for
FLUTE, CLARINET, ALTO SAX, TENOR SAX, TRUMPET,
HORN, TROMBONE, VIOLIN, VIOLA, CELLO

ISBN 978-1-5400-0236-5

The following songs are the property of:

Bourne Co.
Music Publishers
5 West 37th Street
New York, NY 10018

BABY MINE
GIVE A LITTLE WHISTLE
HEIGH-HO
HI-DIDDLE-DEE-DEE (AN ACTOR'S LIFE FOR ME)
I'M WISHING
I'VE GOT NO STRINGS
SOME DAY MY PRINCE WILL COME
WHEN I SEE AN ELEPHANT FLY
WHEN YOU WISH UPON A STAR
WHISTLE WHILE YOU WORK
WHO'S AFRAID OF THE BIG BAD WOLF?
WITH A SMILE AND A SONG

DISTRIBUTED BY

7777 W. BLUEMOUND RD. P.O. BOX 13819 MILWAUKEE, WI 53213

Visit Hal Leonard Online at
www.halleonard.com

CONTENTS

BABY MINE
from DUMBO

TENOR SAX

Words by NED WASHINGTON
Music by FRANK CHURCHILL

THE BALLAD OF DAVY CROCKETT
from DAVY CROCKETT

Words by TOM BLACKBURN
Music by GEORGE BRUNS

BELLA NOTTE
from LADY AND THE TRAMP

Music and Lyrics by PEGGY LEE
and SONNY BURKE

Slowly

BE OUR GUEST
from BEAUTY AND THE BEAST

TENOR SAX

Music by ALAN MENKEN
Lyrics by HOWARD ASHMAN

BEAUTY AND THE BEAST

from BEAUTY AND THE BEAST

TENOR SAX

Music by ALAN MENKEN
Lyrics by HOWARD ASHMAN

Moderately slow

BELLE
from BEAUTY AND THE BEAST

TENOR SAX

Music by ALAN MENKEN
Lyrics by HOWARD ASHMAN

BIBBIDI-BOBBIDI-BOO
(The Magic Song)
from CINDERELLA

Words by JERRY LIVINGSTON
Music by MACK DAVID and AL HOFFMAN

Brightly

BREAKING FREE
from HIGH SCHOOL MUSICAL

TENOR SAX

Words and Music by
JAMIE HOUSTON

Moderately

TENOR SAX

BEST OF FRIENDS
from THE FOX AND THE HOUND

TENOR SAX

Words by STAN FIDEL
Music by RICHARD JOHNSTON

Moderately

CAN YOU FEEL THE LOVE TONIGHT

from THE LION KING

TENOR SAX

Music by ELTON JOHN
Lyrics by TIM RICE

Pop Ballad

CANDLE ON THE WATER

from PETE'S DRAGON

TENOR SAX

Words and Music by AL KASHA
and JOEL HIRSCHHORN

CHIM CHIM CHER-EE

from MARY POPPINS

TENOR SAX

Words and Music by RICHARD M. SHERMAN
and ROBERT B. SHERMAN

Lightly, with gusto

CIRCLE OF LIFE

from THE LION KING

TENOR SAX

Music by ELTON JOHN
Lyrics by TIM RICE

Moderately (with an African beat)

THE CLIMB
from HANNAH MONTANA: THE MOVIE

TENOR SAX

Words and Music by JESSI ALEXANDER
and JON MABE

Moderately slow

CRUELLA DE VIL
from 101 DALMATIANS

TENOR SAX

Words and Music by
MEL LEVEN

A DREAM IS A WISH YOUR HEART MAKES
from CINDERELLA

Words and Music by MACK DAVID,
AL HOFFMAN and JERRY LIVINGSTON

FEED THE BIRDS
(Tuppence a Bag)
from MARY POPPINS

Words and Music by RICHARD M. SHERMAN
and ROBERT B. SHERMAN

COLORS OF THE WIND

from POCAHONTAS

TENOR SAX

Music by ALAN MENKEN
Lyrics by STEPHEN SCHWARTZ

DO YOU WANT TO BUILD A SNOWMAN?

from FROZEN

TENOR SAX

Music and Lyrics by KRISTEN ANDERSON-LOPEZ
and ROBERT LOPEZ

DAYS IN THE SUN

from BEAUTY AND THE BEAST

TENOR SAX

Music by ALAN MENKEN
Lyrics by TIM RICE

Moderately

small notes optional

Slower

EVERMORE
from BEAUTY AND THE BEAST

TENOR SAX

Music by ALAN MENKEN
Lyrics by TIM RICE

HEIGH-HO
(The Dwarfs' Marching Song)
from SNOW WHITE AND THE SEVEN DWARFS

Words by LARRY MOREY
Music by FRANK CHURCHILL

Brightly, cheerfully

FOR THE FIRST TIME IN FOREVER
from FROZEN

TENOR SAX

Music and Lyrics by KRISTEN ANDERSON-LOPEZ
and ROBERT LOPEZ

Moderately, with excitement

Moderately, with expression

With excitement

With expression

HI-DIDDLE-DEE-DEE
(An Actor's Life for Me)
from PINOCCHIO

Words by NED WASHINGTON
Music by LEIGH HARLINE

Brightly, in 2

FRIEND LIKE ME

from ALADDIN

TENOR SAX

Music by ALAN MENKEN
Lyrics by HOWARD ASHMAN

GASTON
from BEAUTY AND THE BEAST

TENOR SAX

Music by ALAN MENKEN
Lyrics by HOWARD ASHMAN

Moderately slow, in 1

GOD HELP THE OUTCASTS

from THE HUNCHBACK OF NOTRE DAME

TENOR SAX

Music by ALAN MENKEN
Lyrics by STEPHEN SCHWARTZ

Slowly

GIVE A LITTLE WHISTLE
from PINOCCHIO

Words by NED WASHINGTON
Music by LEIGH HARLINE

Moderately, in 2

GO THE DISTANCE
from HERCULES

TENOR SAX

Music by ALAN MENKEN
Lyrics by DAVID ZIPPEL

HAKUNA MATATA

from THE LION KING

TENOR SAX

Music by ELTON JOHN
Lyrics by TIM RICE

HAPPY WORKING SONG
from ENCHANTED

TENOR SAX

Music by ALAN MENKEN
Lyrics by STEPHEN SCHWARTZ

HE'S A PIRATE
from PIRATES OF THE CARIBBEAN: THE CURSE OF THE BLACK PEARL

TENOR SAX

Music by KLAUS BADELT,
GEOFFREY ZANELLI and HANS ZIMMER

HE'S A TRAMP
from LADY AND THE TRAMP

Words and Music by PEGGY LEE
and SONNY BURKE

HOW DOES A MOMENT LAST FOREVER
from BEAUTY AND THE BEAST

TENOR SAX

Music by ALAN MENKEN
Lyrics by TIM RICE

I JUST CAN'T WAIT TO BE KING

from THE LION KING

TENOR SAX

Music by ELTON JOHN
Lyrics by TIM RICE

Bright Two-beat

HOW FAR I'LL GO
from MOANA

TENOR SAX

Music and Lyrics by
LIN-MANUEL MIRANDA

Moderately, in 2

I'M LATE
from ALICE IN WONDERLAND

Words by BOB HILLIARD
Music by SAMMY FAIN

Moderately fast

I SEE THE LIGHT

from TANGLED

TENOR SAX

Music by ALAN MENKEN
Lyrics by GLENN SLATER

I'M WISHING
from SNOW WHITE AND THE SEVEN DWARFS

Words by LARRY MOREY
Music by FRANK CHURCHILL

I'LL MAKE A MAN OUT OF YOU

from MULAN

TENOR SAX

Music by MATTHEW WILDER
Lyrics by DAVID ZIPPEL

Moderately

IN SUMMER
from FROZEN

TENOR SAX

Music and Lyrics by KRISTEN ANDERSON-LOPEZ
and ROBERT LOPEZ

Moderately, in 2

I'VE GOT A DREAM
from TANGLED

TENOR SAX

Music by ALAN MENKEN
Lyrics by GLENN SLATER

IF I CAN'T LOVE HER

from BEAUTY AND THE BEAST: THE BROADWAY MUSICAL

TENOR SAX

Music by ALAN MENKEN
Lyrics by TIM RICE

TENOR SAX

IF I NEVER KNEW YOU

(End Title)

from POCAHONTAS

TENOR SAX

Music by ALAN MENKEN
Lyrics by STEPHEN SCHWARTZ

Moderately slow

I'VE GOT NO STRINGS
from PINOCCHIO

TENOR SAX

Words by NED WASHINGTON
Music by LEIGH HARLINE

Quickly, joyfully

IT'S A SMALL WORLD
from Disney Parks' "it's a small world" attraction

Words and Music by RICHARD M. SHERMAN
and ROBERT B. SHERMAN

KISS THE GIRL
from THE LITTLE MERMAID

TENOR SAX

Music by ALAN MENKEN
Lyrics by HOWARD ASHMAN

LAVA
from LAVA

TENOR SAX

Music and Lyrics by
JAMES FORD MURPHY

Moderately slow, in 2

LOVE IS AN OPEN DOOR
from FROZEN

TENOR SAX

Music and Lyrics by KRISTEN ANDERSON-LOPEZ
and ROBERT LOPEZ

LET IT GO
from FROZEN

TENOR SAX

Music and Lyrics by KRISTEN ANDERSON-LOPEZ
and ROBERT LOPEZ

Slowly, in 2

TENOR SAX

LAVENDER BLUE
(Dilly Dilly)
from SO DEAR TO MY HEART

Words by LARRY MOREY
Music by ELIOT DANIEL

MICKEY MOUSE MARCH
from THE MICKEY MOUSE CLUB

Words and Music by
JIMMIE DODD

LET'S GO FLY A KITE

from MARY POPPINS

Words and Music by RICHARD M. SHERMAN
and ROBERT B. SHERMAN

With gusto

THE LORD IS GOOD TO ME
from MELODY TIME

TENOR SAX

Words and Music by KIM GANNON
and WALTER KENT

MY FUNNY FRIEND AND ME
from THE EMPEROR'S NEW GROOVE

Lyrics by STING
Music by STING and DAVID HARTLEY

TENOR SAX

PART OF YOUR WORLD

from THE LITTLE MERMAID

TENOR SAX

Music by ALAN MENKEN
Lyrics by HOWARD ASHMAN

MOTHER KNOWS BEST

from TANGLED

TENOR SAX

Music by ALAN MENKEN
Lyrics by GLENN SLATER

A PIRATE'S LIFE

from PETER PAN

Words by ED PENNER
Music by OLIVER WALLACE

RUMBLY IN MY TUMBLY
from THE MANY ADVENTURES OF WINNIE THE POOH

Words and Music by RICHARD M. SHERMAN
and ROBERT B. SHERMAN

REFLECTION
from MULAN

TENOR SAX

Music by MATTHEW WILDER
Lyrics by DAVID ZIPPEL

Moderately slow

THE SECOND STAR TO THE RIGHT
from PETER PAN

Words by SAMMY CAHN
Music by SAMMY FAIN

SEIZE THE DAY
from NEWSIES

TENOR SAX

Music by ALAN MENKEN
Lyrics by JACK FELDMAN

SO THIS IS LOVE
from CINDERELLA

TENOR SAX

Words and Music by AL HOFFMAN,
MACK DAVID and JERRY LIVINGSTON

SO CLOSE
from ENCHANTED

TENOR SAX

Music by ALAN MENKEN
Lyrics by STEPHEN SCHWARTZ

Moderately slow, in 4

Slowly, freely

THE SIAMESE CAT SONG

from LADY AND THE TRAMP

TENOR SAX

Words and Music by PEGGY LEE
and SONNY BURKE

Slowly

SOME DAY MY PRINCE WILL COME

from SNOW WHITE AND THE SEVEN DWARFS

Words by LARRY MOREY
Music by FRANK CHURCHILL

Moderately

SOMEDAY
from THE HUNCHBACK OF NOTRE DAME

TENOR SAX

Music by ALAN MENKEN
Lyrics by STEPHEN SCHWARTZ

SOMETHING THERE
from BEAUTY AND THE BEAST

TENOR SAX

Music by ALAN MENKEN
Lyrics by HOWARD ASHMAN

A SPOONFUL OF SUGAR
from MARY POPPINS

TENOR SAX

Words and Music by RICHARD M. SHERMAN
and ROBERT B. SHERMAN

SUPERCALIFRAGILISTICEXPIALIDOCIOUS

from MARY POPPINS

TENOR SAX

Words and Music by RICHARD M. SHERMAN
and ROBERT B. SHERMAN

"THIS IS ME."
from RATATOUILLE

TENOR SAX

Music by MICHAEL GIACCHINO

THAT'S HOW YOU KNOW
from ENCHANTED

TENOR SAX

Music by ALAN MENKEN
Lyrics by STEPHEN SCHWARTZ

TOYLAND MARCH
from BABES IN TOYLAND

Adapted from V. HERBERT Melody
Words by MEL LEVEN
Music by GEORGE BRUNS

March tempo

TRASHIN' THE CAMP

(Pop Version)

from TARZAN™

TENOR SAX

Words and Music by
PHIL COLLINS

THE UNBIRTHDAY SONG

from ALICE IN WONDERLAND

TENOR SAX

Words and Music by MACK DAVID,
AL HOFFMAN and JERRY LIVINGSTON

Brightly

TRUE LOVE'S KISS
from ENCHANTED

TENOR SAX

Music by ALAN MENKEN
Lyrics by STEPHEN SCHWARTZ

WESTWARD HO, THE WAGONS!
from WESTWARD HO, THE WAGONS!

Words by TOM BLACKBURN
Music by GEORGE BRUNS

WE BELONG TOGETHER
from TOY STORY 3

TENOR SAX

Music and Lyrics by
RANDY NEWMAN

WHEN I SEE AN ELEPHANT FLY

from DUMBO

Words by NED WASHINGTON
Music by OLIVER WALLACE

Moderately fast

WE KNOW THE WAY
from MOANA

TENOR SAX

Music by OPETAIA FOA'I
Lyrics by OPETAIA FOA'I
and LIN-MANUEL MIRANDA

Moderately

A WHALE OF A TALE
from 20,000 LEAGUES UNDER THE SEA

TENOR SAX

Words and Music by NORMAN GIMBEL
and AL HOFFMAN

With a bounce

WE'RE ALL IN THIS TOGETHER

from HIGH SCHOOL MUSICAL

TENOR SAX

Words and Music by MATTHEW GERRARD
and ROBBIE NEVIL

WHISTLE WHILE YOU WORK
from SNOW WHITE AND THE SEVEN DWARFS

Words by LARRY MOREY
Music by FRANK CHURCHILL

WHEN SHE LOVED ME

from TOY STORY 2

TENOR SAX

Music and Lyrics by
RANDY NEWMAN

Tenderly, very freely

WHEN YOU WISH UPON A STAR

from PINOCCHIO

TENOR SAX

Words by NED WASHINGTON
Music by LEIGH HARLINE

Moderately

WHEN WILL MY LIFE BEGIN?

from TANGLED

TENOR SAX

Music by ALAN MENKEN
Lyrics by GLENN SLATER

Moderately slow (in 4)

Slowly, freely

WITH A SMILE AND A SONG
from SNOW WHITE AND THE SEVEN DWARFS

Words by LARRY MOREY
Music by FRANK CHURCHILL

Moderately slow, in 2

WHO'S AFRAID OF THE BIG BAD WOLF?

from THREE LITTLE PIGS

TENOR SAX

Words and Music by
FRANK CHURCHILL
Additional Lyric by ANN RONELL

Moderately, in 2

WINNIE THE POOH
from THE MANY ADVENTURES OF WINNIE THE POOH

Tenor Sax

Words and Music by RICHARD M. SHERMAN
and ROBERT B. SHERMAN

A WHOLE NEW WORLD

from ALADDIN

TENOR SAX

Music by ALAN MENKEN
Lyrics by TIM RICE

THE WONDERFUL THING ABOUT TIGGERS

Tenor Sax

from THE MANY ADVENTURES OF WINNIE THE POOH

Words and Music by RICHARD M. SHERMAN
and ROBERT B. SHERMAN

Very brightly

YO HO

(A Pirate's Life for Me)

from Disney Parks' Pirates of the Caribbean attraction

Words by XAVIER ATENCIO
Music by GEORGE BRUNS

In a robust manner

THEME FROM ZORRO
from the Television Series

Words by NORMAN FOSTER
Music by GEORGE BRUNS

Moderately, in 2

WRITTEN IN THE STARS

from AIDA

TENOR SAX

Music by ELTON JOHN
Lyrics by TIM RICE

YOU CAN FLY! YOU CAN FLY! YOU CAN FLY!

TENOR SAX

from PETER PAN

Words by SAMMY CAHN
Music by SAMMY FAIN

YOU ARE THE MUSIC IN ME

from HIGH SCHOOL MUSICAL 2

TENOR SAX

Words and Music by
JAMIE HOUSTON

Moderately fast Rock

YOU'LL BE IN MY HEART
(Pop Version)
from TARZAN™

TENOR SAX

Words and Music by
PHIL COLLINS

YOU'RE WELCOME
from MOANA

TENOR SAX

Music and Lyrics by
LIN-MANUEL MIRANDA

ZIP-A-DEE-DOO-DAH
from SONG OF THE SOUTH

Words by RAY GILBERT
Music by ALLIE WRUBEL

ZERO TO HERO
from HERCULES

TENOR SAX

Music by ALAN MENKEN
Lyrics by DAVID ZIPPEL

Driving 4

D.C. al Coda

CODA

YOU'VE GOT A FRIEND IN ME

from TOY STORY

TENOR SAX

Music and Lyrics by
RANDY NEWMAN

Easy Shuffle